QUICK PRACTICE
WRITING SKILLS
Grades 4–5

Dozens of Reproducible Pages
That Give Kids Practice
in Grammar, Mechanics, Spelling,
and Other Key Writing Skills

by Marcia Miller and Martin Lee

NEW YORK • TORONTO • LONDON • AUKLAND • SYDNEY
MEXICO CITY • NEW DELHI • HONG KONG • BUENOS AIRES

SCHOLASTIC
Teaching
Resources

Cover design by Maria Lilja
Cover illustration by Mike Gordon
Interior design by Jeffrey Dorman
Interior illustrations by Margeaux Lucas

ISBN 0-439-37096-5
Copyright © 2003 by Marcia Miller and Martin Lee
All rights reserved.
Printed in the U.S.A.

1 2 3 4 5 6 7 8 9 10   40   09 08 07 06 05 04 03

CONTENTS

ABOUT THIS BOOK

As teachers, we want to guide students to become good writers, to empower them to communicate in writing as freely, naturally, and effectively as they do when speaking.

> **Quick Practice Writing Skills: Grades 4–5** is one of a series of four grade-specific books for students K–8. Each book has a dual purpose—to sharpen students' skills as writers, and to provide ways you can help to prepare them for success when they take standardized tests of writing.

Because writing is such a crucial measure of one's ability to communicate, many school districts and state departments of education utilize approved lists of writing standards at each grade level that students are expected to meet. Writing has increasingly become a regular component of standardized testing. In addition to short-answer items, standardized tests ask students to plan, write, edit, and present a finished piece of independent writing on a given topic.

> **Quick Practice Writing Skills: Grades 4–5** gives students opportunities to practice and develop some of the key skills and strategies of the writing process. By using this book, your students will grow as writers.

Good writing doesn't happen by chance. We become skilled writers because we write—and keep on writing. We write to express fact, opinion, humor, memory, feelings, admiration, criticism, and creativity. We write to instruct, inform, and interpret. The more we write, the more we understand about writing. We learn to mold a piece of writing to a given purpose, to fit a particular audience, and to achieve a certain result.

> **Quick Practice Writing Skills: Grades 4–5** addresses the many ways that standardized tests may evaluate students' ability to express themselves as writers.

The activity pages you will find in *Quick Practice Writing Skills: Grades 4–5* are based on recent versions of an assortment of testing instruments, as well as a compilation of standards applied to language arts and writing. They provide various formats and levels of complexity within the targeted grade range. Each page or activity is self-contained and concise enough to be used as a warm-up or follow-up to a related lesson within your writing curriculum. While some activity pages have questions with only one correct answer, others are open-ended, mirroring many of the newer standardized tests.

In developing these books, we have drawn upon a wide range of materials and resources. One very useful Web site you may wish to explore can be found at **www.mcrel.org**. Here, you can examine a wealth of materials about standards-based education in general as well as specific curriculum standards, testing, and position papers.

> **Quick Practice Writing Skills: Grades 4–5** can help your students develop greater confidence and feel more relaxed in a test-taking situation.

Test taking is like any task—the more it is practiced, the less daunting it becomes. The activities in this book cannot substitute for the standardized testing instruments your students will take, as mandated by your school district and/or state education department. But they can decrease some of the anxiety and mystery surrounding standards and standardized testing.

USING THIS BOOK

Quick Practice Writing Skills: Grades 4–5 has been organized into four main sections that reflect the general aspects of writing:

> **1. Conventions of Grammar and Mechanics**
>
> **2. Writing Styles**
>
> **3. The Writing Process**
>
> **4. Writing Activities**

Within each section, we address a particular aspect of writing in quantifiable and grade-appropriate ways. Obviously, in a book of this length, it is not possible to test everything, nor can one book be certain to dovetail with every aspect of your particular writing curriculum or the standards your students are expected to meet. Simply regard the sections as broad-stroke plans of organization.

Standardized writing tests include short-answer and free-form writing tasks. In this book we include both. You will find certain writing skills exercised in short-answer items. You will also find ample opportunities for open-ended writing, especially in section 4.

At the back of the book, you will find a reproducible "bubble sheet," which gives students practice using a common standardized test format, and a Writer's Self-Evaluation Checklist, which students can use as an aid to refine their writing. You will also find selected answers and brief teacher notes.

Here are some suggestions for using Quick Practice Writing Skills: Grades 4–5

- Present the activity pages in any order you wish.

- Allow pages to be completed independently, in pairs, in small groups, or by the whole class as a group activity. Use your best judgment.

- You may want to read directions aloud to remove a potential stumbling block for less-independent readers.

- You may wish to do a sample exercise together, as you see fit.

- Feel free to take any format we provide in this book and revise it to fit your students' needs. Use any exercise as a springboard for similar activities you create, or extend and develop it into a complete lesson or project.

- Take the time to review and discuss students' responses. Analyze the responses for diagnostic use.

- Print and distribute (or post) the Tried & True Test-Taking Tips on page 6. Discuss them with your class and invite students to add their own useful suggestions to the list.

TRIED & TRUE TEST-TAKING TIPS

- Get plenty of rest the night before the test.

- Eat a healthy breakfast.

- Wear comfortable clothing.

- Get to school on time!

- Gather all the materials you need—sharp pencils, erasers, scratch paper, and so on.

- Bring your positive attitude!

- Listen to or read instructions carefully.

- If you don't understand something, raise your hand and ask for help.

- Work purposefully and carefully.

- Read the whole question and all the given answer choices before marking anything.

- Don't let other people distract you. Stick to the task.

- Try to answer ALL questions. But if you are stumped, take a deep breath and move on. Come back to the question later.

- If you change your mind, erase your first answer completely.

- If you aren't sure, choose the answer that seems best to you.

- Double-check your answers, if you have time.

- Proofread your writing.

- Neatness counts! Make sure that all your writing is legible.

PART 1:

CONVENTIONS OF GRAMMAR AND MECHANICS

Name ....

FIND THE NOUN

Mark the letter beneath the word that is a noun.

1. The world's first toothbrushes weren't brushes at all.
Ⓐ   Ⓑ   Ⓒ   Ⓓ

2. They were pencil-sized twigs that were frayed at one end.
Ⓐ   Ⓑ Ⓒ   Ⓓ

3. These "chew sticks" were found in many ancient Egyptian tombs!
Ⓐ   Ⓑ Ⓒ   Ⓓ

4. The oldest bristle toothbrush was made in China over 500 years ago.
Ⓐ   Ⓑ Ⓒ   Ⓓ

5. The stiff bristles came from the necks of hogs.
Ⓐ   Ⓑ   Ⓒ   Ⓓ

6. They were attached to handles carved out of bone or bamboo.
Ⓐ   Ⓑ   Ⓒ   Ⓓ

7. The early Chinese toothbrushes were known for having hard bristles.
Ⓐ   Ⓑ   Ⓒ   Ⓓ

8. Europeans who brushed at all used softer toothbrushes made of horsehair.
Ⓐ   Ⓑ   Ⓒ   Ⓓ

9. A 1723 French medical book said to clean teeth with a natural sponge.
Ⓐ   Ⓑ   Ⓒ   Ⓓ

10. But any natural animal hair could introduce germs to the mouth.
Ⓐ   Ⓑ   Ⓒ   Ⓓ

11. In 1938, Americans could buy the very first nylon-bristled toothbrush.
Ⓐ   Ⓑ   Ⓒ   Ⓓ

12. Nylon was a new fiber that was considered safer and cleaner to use.
Ⓐ   Ⓑ   Ⓒ   Ⓓ

13. Today, you can get toothbrushes in any size, stiffness, shape, and color.
Ⓐ Ⓑ   Ⓒ   Ⓓ

14. You can also get electric toothbrushes to help keep your mouth healthy.
Ⓐ   Ⓑ   Ⓒ   Ⓓ

Name ....

NOUN NAMES

Each sentence has a noun shown in **boldface**.
Write whether that noun names a *person*, a *place*, a *thing*, or an *idea*.

1. Many people think that the koala is a

   kind of **bear**. _____

2. But **scientists** know that koalas

   are not bears. _____

3. In fact, koalas are marsupials—mammals

   with a **pouch**. _____

4. Most of the world's koalas live in **Australia**. _____

5. The **koala** is a tree-dwelling plant eater. _____

6. Koalas find **safety** living high up in the branches. _____

7. Have you read *The World of the Koala* by **Melvin** Lee? _____

8. Koalas have several forms of **communication**. _____

9. Their **sounds** include bellowing, humming, and crying. _____

10. Koalas spend about 18 to 20 hours a **day** resting. _____

11. **Australians** observe Save the Koala Month each July. _____

12. At **Koala Beach,** humans and koalas can live side by side.

_____

WRITE THE PLURAL

Fill in the chart below by making the singular nouns plural.
The first one has been done for you.

	ONE...	MANY...
1.	bear	bears
2.	worker	
3.	table	
4.	branch	
5.	box	
6.	pony	
7.	lady	
8.	monkey	
9.	cliff	
10.	shelf	
11.	life	
12.	hero	
13.	radio	
14.	mouse	
15.	ox	
16.	sheep	

WRITE THE SINGULAR

Fill in the chart below by making the plural nouns singular.
The first one has been done for you.

	LOTS OF...	BUT ONLY ONE...
1.	lamps	lamp
2.	stages	
3.	inches	
4.	wishes	
5.	taxes	
6.	countries	
7.	cherries	
8.	journeys	
9.	elves	
10.	loaves	
11.	echoes	
12.	zeroes	
13.	autos	
14.	men	
15.	deer	

FINISH THE SENTENCE

Write the correct form of the noun in **boldface** to finish each sentence. The first one has been done for you.

1. First I saw only one **bunny**, but now I see five ___bunnies___ .

2. We asked six **men**, but only one _____ was able to help.

3. Most **buses** were crowded, but my _____ was almost empty.

4. I need only one **wish**, but the genie gave me three _____ .

5. The lone **wolf** howling at the moon didn't sound like the pack of

_____ we saw at the zoo.

6. There are many **solos** to learn, but her _____ is the longest.

7. After peeling **potatoes** all morning, the cook was glad to finish the

very last _____ .

8. The janitor carries lots of **keys**, but only one special _____

unlocks the grand piano.

9. I had my first loose **tooth** when I was five, but by now I've lost all

my baby _____ .

10. The old bull **moose** led a pack of seven _____

across the meadow.

Name ....

COMMON NOUNS, PROPER NOUNS

Write a proper noun that is an example of each common noun.
The first one has been done for you.

1. state _____Arizona_____

2. singer _____

3. river _____

4. artist _____

5. woman _____

6. mountain _____

7. athlete _____

8. game _____

9. shampoo _____

10. song _____

11. medicine _____

12. doctor _____

Write a common noun to name the group that includes each
proper noun. The first one has been done for you.

13. Brazil _____country_____

14. Harry Potter _____

15. New York Mets _____

16. Asia _____

17. Britney Spears _____

18. Honda _____

19. *Lord of the Rings* _____

20. Indiana _____

21. Superior _____

22. April _____

23. Tuesday _____

24. Abe Lincoln _____

Name ....

IDENTIFY KINDS OF NOUNS

Read each phrase. Decide whether the underlined word(s) is a common noun, a proper noun, a collective noun, or not a noun at all. Mark the correct letter.

A = common noun	**B** = proper noun	**C** = collective noun	**D** = not a noun

1. at <u>The Bead Museum</u>   [A] [B] [C] [D]

2. located in the <u>center</u> of Arizona   [A] [B] [C] [D]

3. started by a retired interior <u>decorator</u>   [A] [B] [C] [D]

4. vast <u>collection</u> of jewelry   [A] [B] [C] [D]

5. in the small town of <u>Prescott</u>   [A] [B] [C] [D]

6. <u>visited</u> the research library   [A] [B] [C] [D]

7. examples from nearly every <u>country</u>   [A] [B] [C] [D]

8. made of wood, <u>glass</u>, bone, metal, and stone   [A] [B] [C] [D]

9. can reveal important <u>information</u>   [A] [B] [C] [D]

10. accepted in <u>payment</u>   [A] [B] [C] [D]

11. the <u>Acoma</u> people of New Mexico   [A] [B] [C] [D]

12. <u>used</u> beads for trading purposes   [A] [B] [C] [D]

13. the <u>staff</u> of the museum   [A] [B] [C] [D]

14. unusual <u>Chinese</u> beads   [A] [B] [C] [D]

15. free <u>admission</u> to the museum   [A] [B] [C] [D]

16. on a computer <u>network</u>   [A] [B] [C] [D]

17. assisted by a <u>team</u> of scholars   [A] [B] [C] [D]

18. a lovely wrist <u>ornament</u>   [A] [B] [C] [D]

19. delicate glass beads from <u>Italy</u>   [A] [B] [C] [D]

20. long <u>string</u> of stones   [A] [B] [C] [D]

PICK THE BEST NOUN

Circle the letter of the noun that best completes each sentence.

1. Would you like to join the soccer _____?
   a. field   **b.** song   **c.** ball   **d.** team

2. You can learn how to play the game and have _____, too.
   a. fun   **b.** leaves   **c.** faces   **d.** water

3. We practice every _____ after school at Boyd Park.
   a. April   **b.** Tuesday   **c.** month   **d.** morning

4. We wear cool _____ that say "Dragons" on the back.
   a. cars   **b.** books   **c.** uniforms   **d.** glasses

5. Our _____ is strict, but she is also patient and fair.
   a. ball   **b.** coach   **c.** dragon   **d.** team

6. Sometimes at the end of practice, we watch _____ of famous soccer games.
   a. players   **b.** women   **c.** videos   **d.** songs

7. It's really exciting to play before a cheering _____.
   a. tent   **b.** crowd   **c.** street   **d.** rabbit

8. After a game, we usually share a _____ before we go home.
   a. dollar   **b.** poem   **c.** rose   **d.** snack

9. If we win, we might get our picture in the _____.
   a. paper   **b.** camera   **c.** freezer   **d.** locker

10. Of all the _____ you can play, we think soccer is the best.
   a. tapes   **b.** sports   **c.** radios   **d.** heroes

PICK THE PRONOUN

Circle the letter of the pronoun that best completes each sentence.

1. The wet children left _____ drippy umbrellas hanging on the porch rail.
   a. his   **b.** their   **c.** her   **d.** they

2. Soon, each umbrella had a good-sized puddle beneath _____ .
   a. her   **b.** they   **c.** it   **d.** him

3. Inside, _____ mother handed them fluffy towels.
   a. us   **b.** your   **c.** she   **d.** their

4. "Now, dry _____ feet before you dirty up the rug," she reminded them.
   a. my   **b.** our   **c.** your   **d.** yours

5. "Gee, _____ is the worst rain storm all spring," the children remarked.
   a. these   **b.** them   **c.** they   **d.** this

6. "I hope that old storm cloud lets go of all _____ water by tonight," said Jim.
   a. it   **b.** his   **c.** our   **d.** its

7. "If not, _____ class trip to the fort tomorrow may be cancelled," said Kelly.
   a. ours   **b.** our   **c.** its   **d.** they

8. The fort, _____ was high on a hill, would be too muddy and slippery.
   a. whom   **b.** whose   **c.** who   **d.** which

9. The children went to _____ computer and checked a local weather site.
   a. their   **b.** your   **c.** they   **d.** what

10. "It says CLEAR for tomorrow. I sure hope the forecasters know what _____ are talking about," said Kelly.
   a. its   **b.** their   **c.** them   **d.** they

Name ....

PRONOUNS AND ANTECEDENTS

Mark the correct *antecedent* (the noun that matches the meaning) of each underlined pronoun.

1. Checkers is a very old game; <u>it</u> was played in Egypt over 4,000 years ago!

   (A) **board game**   (C) **checkers**

   (B) **Egypt**   (D) **years**

2. Players then were neither children nor old folks; <u>they</u> were warriors and rulers.

   (A) **players**   (C) **folks**

   (B) **children**   (D) **warriors**

3. What proof do we have for checkers in Egypt? <u>It</u> appears in ancient paintings.

   (A) **ancient**   (C) **paintings**

   (B) **proof**   (D) **Egypt**

4. "Enemy" pieces were "captured" by opponents <u>who</u> tried to defeat each other.

   (A) **enemy**   (C) **opponents**

   (B) **pieces**   (D) **other**

5. Another name for checkers is "draughts." <u>This</u> is pronounced *drafts*.

   (A) **name**   (C) **drafts**

   (B) **draughts**   (D) **checkers**

6. Many famous people through history loved to play checkers. <u>One</u> was Ulysses S. Grant—the Civil War general who later became president.

   (A) **general**   (C) **famous person**

   (B) **president**   (D) **history**

7. The oldest known book about checkers (draughts) was published in Spain in 1547. <u>Its</u> author was Antonio Torquemada.

   (A) **the book's**   (C) **the game's**

   (B) **the author's**   (D) **Spain's**

8. The world's largest checkerboard, <u>which</u> uses big round pillows for playing pieces, is in Petal, Mississippi.

   (A) **pieces**   (C) **pillows**

   (B) **Mississippi**   (D) **checkerboard**

Name ....

CHECK THE PRONOUN

Read each sentence. Check the pronoun usage. If there is no error,
circle *Correct*. If there is an error, circle *Incorrect*.

1. Her bicycle has ten gears, but mine
bicycle has fifteen.

      Correct   **Incorrect**

2. Which brand is your bicycle?

      Correct   **Incorrect**

3. I want a mountain bike, but me dad says
it costs too much.

      Correct   **Incorrect**

4. If I can save the money, maybe I can buy
one next summer.

      Correct   **Incorrect**

5. At the bike race, us sat right by the finish line.

      Correct   **Incorrect**

6. The members of the cycling team wear numbers on its jersey.

      Correct   **Incorrect**

7. We cheered for everybody, but us secretly hoped Rico would win.

      Correct   **Incorrect**

8. He and me used to ride around together on weekends.

      Correct   **Incorrect**

9. Rico wears weights on he legs to build his muscles.

      Correct   **Incorrect**

10. Cycling first appeared in the 1896 Olympics, who were
held in Athens, Greece.

      Correct   **Incorrect**

11. That race was short, compared to cycling races today.

      Correct   **Incorrect**

12. Have you ever seen a velodrome? It is an indoor arena
whose walls are sloped for cycling races.

      Correct   **Incorrect**

Name ....

FIND THE VERB

Mark the letter beneath the word that is a verb.

1. Did you know that bats are the only mammals
         Ⓐ   Ⓑ   Ⓒ

that can fly?
     Ⓓ

2. Many people fear bats, but bats are really
       Ⓐ   Ⓑ   Ⓒ

very important to us.
        Ⓓ

3. Bats eat half their body weight in bugs every night.
     Ⓐ   Ⓑ   Ⓒ   Ⓓ

4. Fear and ignorance give people the wrong ideas about bats.
     Ⓐ   Ⓑ Ⓒ   Ⓓ

5. Most bats are harmless to humans and valuable to nature's balance.
        Ⓐ   Ⓑ   Ⓒ   Ⓓ

6. Bat mothers generally produce only one baby (called a pup) each year.
     Ⓐ   Ⓑ   Ⓒ   Ⓓ

7. Bats usually live in large colonies, often in caves or other dark places.
      Ⓐ Ⓑ   Ⓒ   Ⓓ

8. Each year, vandals destroy thousands of bats by blocking cave entrances.
        Ⓐ   Ⓑ   Ⓒ   Ⓓ

9. Bats are not really blind, but they do have that reputation.
      Ⓐ   Ⓑ Ⓒ   Ⓓ

10. As for the belief that bats carry rabies, this idea has been exaggerated.
     Ⓐ   Ⓑ   Ⓒ   Ⓓ

11. You're more likely to be hit by a falling star than to get rabies from a bat.
       Ⓐ   Ⓑ   Ⓒ   Ⓓ

12. All the people who misunderstand bats keep science educators busy!
        Ⓐ   Ⓑ   Ⓒ   Ⓓ

PICK THE VERB FORM

Circle the letter of the verb form that best completes the sentence.

1. Jenny and I decided to _____ members of the camera club.
a. become **b.** becoming **c.** became

2. We _____ meetings twice a week—on Tuesday and Saturdays.
a. has **b.** have **c.** having

3. Our advisor _____ once a photojournalist in Chicago.
a. were **b.** will **c.** was

4. Some of his pictures _____ in newspapers and magazines.
a. appeared **b.** appear **c.** appearing

5. Our advisor has _____ some famous people through his work.
a. know **b.** knew **c.** known

6. Each member may also _____ a digital camera to use.
a. borrowed **b.** borrowing **c.** borrow

7. We _____ so lucky to be able to use such good equipment.
a. be **b.** is **c.** are

8. We are _____ to capture a scene to make it interesting.
a. learned **b.** learn **c.** learning

9. We _____ to mount a photo show next May to show our best work.
a. plan **b.** planned **c.** plans

10. Each of us can _____ our five favorite pictures for the show.
a. chose **b.** choose **c.** choice

11. The evening will _____ with a short skit about photography.
a. begun **b.** began **c.** begin

12. We hope you can _____ to the party where we will celebrate together.
a. coming **b.** came **c.** come

Name ....

USE LINKING VERBS

The most common linking verb is *be*.
Mark the correct form of *be* for each sentence.

1. Last spring, my brother and I _____ helping Uncle Rusty, who is a rancher.

- (A) **are**
- (C) **were**
- (B) **was**
- (D) **have been**

2. The first day we got there—it _____ a Friday—one of his mares had a new foal.

- (A) **has been**
- (C) **may be**
- (B) **was**
- (D) **was being**

3. That was the first time I _____ so close to such a big newborn animal.

- (A) **being**
- (C) **were**
- (B) **have been**
- (D) **had been**

4. Just before the birth, the mother horse _____ quietly pacing in her stall.

- (A) **had been**
- (C) **were**
- (B) **has been**
- (D) **would be**

5. The newborn's wobbly legs _____ longer than its body, yet the baby stood right up.

- (A) **are**
- (C) **were**
- (B) **was**
- (D) **have been**

6. "That's always the way it _____ with newborn foals," said Uncle Rusty with a smile.

- (A) **should be**
- (C) **might be**
- (B) **have been**
- (D) **were**

7. "By summer, that foal _____ a frisky young horse racing its mom," he added.

- (A) **was**
- (C) **were**
- (B) **would be**
- (D) **have been**

8. We had such a great time on the ranch, Uncle Rusty predicted that we _____ back soon.

- (A) **was**
- (C) **were**
- (B) **would be**
- (D) **have been**

Name ....

USE THE VERB

Write a sentence using the verb given.

1. spread _____

_____

_____

2. attend _____

_____

_____

3. understands _____

_____

_____

4. meant _____

_____

_____

5. slept _____

_____

_____

6. will keep _____

_____

_____

USE VERB TENSES

Write the correct form of the verb in **boldface** to finish each sentence. The first one has been done for you.

1. Yesterday I **fed** the cat tuna, but today I will ____feed____ her liver.

2. At last year's water balloon fight, Jack **broke** only two balloons. This year, he hopes to _____ all six of them!

3. Today Jed **draws** with pastels, but yesterday he _____ with markers.

4. Can you **hang** this painting as high as the one we _____ over there?

5. Peg **sleeps** on the top bunk tonight since Jill _____ there last night.

6. Ed **spent** his allowance on candy, but I'll _____ mine only on books.

7. Claire **leaves** for the bus early, but I don't _____ until almost nine.

8. Greg **grew** two inches this summer, but I haven't _____ an inch since spring!

9. I **thought** the movie was much too sad. What did you _____?

10. He has **written** a fine story—far better than the one I _____.

Name ....

USE A BETTER VERB

These sentences have plain verbs. Rewrite each sentence using an exciting verb.

1. Karen <u>ran</u> to the bus stop.

_____

2. The thirsty athlete <u>drank</u> some cool water.

_____

3. Marco <u>walked</u> past the sleeping baby.

_____

4. The lost hikers <u>called</u> for help.

_____

5. When coyotes howl, rabbits <u>go</u> into the nearest hole.

_____

6. Aunt Clara loves to <u>make</u> fancy salads.

_____

7. After the game, Fran <u>sat</u> on a shady bench.

_____

8. "Where did I leave my backpack?" <u>said</u> Dan.

_____

FIND THE ADJECTIVE

Mark the letter beneath the word that is an adjective.

1. The world's tropical rain forests are
                          Ⓐ   Ⓑ

amazing places.
Ⓒ   Ⓓ

2. Rain forests grow so lush because
                  Ⓐ   Ⓑ

of plentiful rain and warm sun.
      Ⓒ   Ⓓ

3. They are home to exotic creatures that live
       Ⓐ   Ⓑ   Ⓒ

nowhere else on earth.
   Ⓓ

4. Rain forests also play an important role in the world's weather.
   Ⓐ   Ⓑ   Ⓒ   Ⓓ

5. The highest part of the rain forest is called the canopy.
   Ⓐ   ⒷⒸ   Ⓓ

6. The canopy contains the most colorful layer of rain forest life.
Ⓐ   Ⓑ   Ⓒ   Ⓓ

7. There are brilliant flowers and fruits of every color.
  Ⓐ   Ⓑ   ⒸⒹ

8. Many rain-forest plants reach enormous sizes that may seem unbelievable.
 Ⓐ   Ⓑ   Ⓒ   Ⓓ

9. The most spectacular of the rain forest's creatures are its birds.
  Ⓐ Ⓑ   Ⓒ   Ⓓ

10. But insects win the grand prize—there are millions of insects in rain forests.
 Ⓐ   Ⓑ   ⒸⒹ

11. Some of the world's most valuable medicines come from rain-forest plants.
      Ⓐ   Ⓑ   Ⓒ   Ⓓ

12. The rosy periwinkle is a plant used to make cancer medicines.
  Ⓐ Ⓑ   Ⓒ   Ⓓ

13. Let's save the rain forests so that future generations can benefit from them.
 Ⓐ Ⓑ   Ⓒ   Ⓓ

Name ....

MAKE COMPARISONS

Write the correct form of the adjective shown in **boldface** to complete each sentence. The first one has been done for you.

1. Carl is certainly a **swift** runner, but Jesse is even ___swifter___.

2. Gary is **younger** than Troy, but Rob is the _____ of all.

3. An eagle is a **large** bird, but an ostrich is far _____.

4. Vanilla ice cream is **good**, but add hot fudge and it's far _____.

5. I thought Chapter 1 was **bad**, but then the book

got even _____.

6. Your cereal has **more** raisins than his, but mine has the _____.

7. If a shiny penny is **lucky**, is a shiny nickel five times _____?

8. I was a bit **hungry** an hour ago, but now I'm feeling

much _____.

9. The noise is **worse** than before, but the very _____ is

yet to come.

10. That bread is as _____ as the **flattest** pancake I've ever seen.

11. Everybody makes a **few** errors, but top students make

the _____ of all.

12. I don't mind a **wet** towel, but that one was _____ than usual.

Name ....

USE A BETTER ADJECTIVE

These sentences have boring adjectives. Rewrite each sentence with a more exciting adjective.

1. That cat has **nice** fur.

_____

2. The gardens were **pretty** today.

_____

3. The way they dance is so **cute**.

_____

4. That was a **bad** excuse.

_____

5. We saw a **good** play.

_____

6. The Rocky Mountains are **big**.

_____

7. They had a **fine** time at the picnic.

_____

8. We took one **interesting** tour together.

_____

9. The soup tasted **awful**.

_____

10. What a **great** vacation we had!

_____

ANSWER WITH ADVERBS

Adverbs can tell *when*, *where*, *how*, or *how much*. Answer each question using one or more of the adverbs in the box below. Write in full sentences.

> always
> eagerly
> loudly
> rarely
> slowly
> occasionally
> usually
> very

1. When does it rain in the desert?

_____

_____

_____

2. How do most animals move in the heat?

_____

_____

_____

3. How does a cactus grow? _____

_____

_____

4. How do thirsty creatures drink? _____

_____

_____

5. How much water should you drink when you are in the desert?

_____

_____

USE ADJECTIVES AND ADVERBS

Circle the letter of the answer that best completes each sentence.

1. That is the _____ of the two rocks to climb.

    a. hard   **b.** harder   **c.** hardest   **d.** more harder

2. It has the _____ face of all the beginner's rocks in the area.

    a. smooth   **b.** smoother   **c.** smoothest   **d.** most smoothest

3. Rock climbing is _____ nowadays thanks to high-tech gear.

    a. safer   **c.** most safe

    b. more safer   **d.** safest

4. Climbers wear special shoes that have the _____ grip and give.

    a. great   **c.** greatest

    b. greater   **d.** more greater

5. Beginning climbers _____ retrace their steps to build confidence and skill.

    a. often   **b.** more often   **c.** most often   **d.** oftenest

6. They are told not to go _____ than their trainers tell them to go.

    a. farther   **b.** more far   **c.** farthest   **d.** more farthest

7. Some cities have indoor climbing walls that are _____ than actual rocks.

    a. difficult   **b.** more difficulter   **c.** difficulter   **d.** more difficult

8. The _____ my local indoor climbing wall opens is 6:00 A.M.

    a. early   **b.** earlier   **c.** most early   **d.** earliest

Name ....

WRITE PREPOSITIONAL PHRASES

A *preposition* is a word that helps relate nouns in time and space. Each sentence below has a preposition shown in **boldface**. Finish each sentence by adding a phrase that makes sense. The first one has been done for you.

1. The monkeys ran **along**

the jungle path
_____.

2. These playful creatures scurried **up**

_____.

3. They were up high, but they could see

through _____.

4. A hungry leopard paced eagerly **below**

_____.

5. The monkeys screeched **at** _____.

6. Will the monkeys be safe **from** _____?

7. The sun began to set **behind** _____.

8. The leopard lost interest and took off **toward** _____

_____.

9. With the leopard gone, the monkeys scampered down **to** _____

_____.

10. There, they chased and groomed each other **until** _____

_____.

11. At last, they curled up to sleep **near** _____

_____.

12. And who knows what the monkeys will do tomorrow **for** _____

_____!

Name ....

ADD PREPOSITIONAL PHRASES

Prepositional phrases can help to add details and description. Notice how the underlined prepositional phrase makes the following sentence better.

They left the house early <u>while the street lamps were still shining</u>.

Rewrite each sentence below to make it more descriptive. Add a prepositional phrase anywhere in the sentence that works. The first one has been done for you.

1. Figure skaters practice regularly.

Figure skaters in training

practice regularly.

2. Many skaters practice in the morning.

_____

_____

3. Renting ice time can be very expensive.

_____

4. But it takes repetition to perfect the routines.

_____

5. Ice skaters expect to fall.

_____

6. They wear protective gear.

_____

7. Many skaters practice off the ice.

_____

8. They jump and fall.

_____

FIND SPELLING MISTAKES

Read each sentence. Decide which underlined word is spelled wrong.
Mark the letter beneath that word.

1. You <u>shuld</u> have <u>been</u> <u>busy</u> with your homework.
Ⓐ Ⓑ Ⓒ

2. His <u>shoose</u> were too <u>tight</u> to <u>wear</u>.
Ⓐ Ⓑ Ⓒ

3. Did the <u>security</u> <u>guard</u> let you <u>thrugh</u> the gate?
Ⓐ Ⓑ Ⓒ

4. David works at the <u>animal</u> <u>hospittle</u>, <u>where</u> he cares for birds.
Ⓐ Ⓑ Ⓒ

5. My next-door <u>neibor</u> asked me to help her <u>straighten</u> some <u>pictures</u>.
Ⓐ Ⓑ Ⓒ

6. After <u>getting</u> several hints, our group <u>finely</u> solved the <u>puzzle</u>.
Ⓐ Ⓑ Ⓒ

7. <u>Everyone</u> wanted to read the <u>mistery</u>, but our <u>copy</u> got lost.
Ⓐ Ⓑ Ⓒ

8. I got my own <u>public</u> <u>libary</u> card for my <u>eighth</u> birthday.
Ⓐ Ⓑ Ⓒ

9. The <u>wimmen</u> who work in the <u>cafeteria</u> know every <u>student</u> by name.
Ⓐ Ⓑ Ⓒ

10. If you <u>study</u> the <u>information</u>, you will <u>probally</u> do well on the quiz.
Ⓐ Ⓑ Ⓒ

11. That <u>vanilla</u> <u>desert</u> we made was really <u>creamy</u>.
Ⓐ Ⓑ Ⓒ

12. When Rover <u>buryed</u> the bone, he <u>ruined</u> three <u>tomato</u> plants.
Ⓐ Ⓑ Ⓒ

Name ....

SPELL CHECK

In each row, circle the word that is spelled wrong. If all the words are spelled right, circle *No Mistake*.

1.	finally	quickly	easyly	*No Mistake*
2.	enlarge	garbage	charje	*No Mistake*
3.	polise	spicy	announcing	*No Mistake*
4.	creation	reaktion	election	*No Mistake*
5.	sneeze	neither	receive	*No Mistake*
6.	remane	contain	reign	*No Mistake*
7.	soften	coughing	coupon	*No Mistake*
8.	scallop	skeleton	sqwish	*No Mistake*
9.	trouble	gobbel	bubble	*No Mistake*
10.	pleasure	swetter	weather	*No Mistake*
11.	several	different	remember	*No Mistake*
12.	themselves	yourself	twelfe	*No Mistake*
13.	sugar	shuffle	punnish	*No Mistake*
14.	gerbil	jingull	jersey	*No Mistake*
15.	turky	monkey	wacky	*No Mistake*
16.	chorus	chowder	chizzle	*No Mistake*

PICK THE HOMOPHONE

Some words sound alike but have different spellings and different meanings. Pick the right word for each sentence. Write it on the line.

acts or **ax**	**1.** Pioneers used the _____ for many chores.
brake or **break**	**2.** He warned his little brother not to _____ the toy.
ceiling or **sealing**	**3.** The painter used a ladder to reach the _____.
chili or **chilly**	**4.** Add hot peppers to your _____ to spice it up.
coarse or **course**	**5.** The dog's whiskers feel _____ to the touch.
fair or **fare**	**6.** Students pay a reduced _____ to ride the bus.
flour or **flower**	**7.** The bread recipe requires three cups of _____.
higher or **hire**	**8.** The store needs to _____ some part-time helpers.
heard or **herd**	**9.** Megan _____ an odd sound coming from the roof.
pedal or **petal**	**10.** A beetle is chewing on the _____ of that rose.
ring or **wring**	**11.** Please _____ out your towel before you hang it up.
soar or **sore**	**12.** We watched the jet _____ into the clouds.

WRITE WITH HOMOPHONES

Homophones are words that sound the same, but have different spellings. For example:

She <u>blew</u> on the tea in the <u>blue</u> mug to cool it off.

For each pair of homophones, write a single sentence that contains both words.

1. hear, here

_____

2. which, witch

_____

3. guessed, guest

_____

4. new, knew

_____

5. root, route

_____

6. right, write

_____

7. there, their

_____

8. weather, whether

_____

9. wood, would

_____

10. chews, choose

_____

Name ....

FORM COMPOUND WORDS

A compound word is made of two shorter words.
Shoelace is a compound word made from *shoe + lace*.

Match a word in List A with another word in List B to make five compound words. Use each word only once. Write your compound words on lines 1 through 5.

LIST A	LIST B
brain	back
quarter	berry
screw	color
straw	driver
water	storm

1. _____

2. _____

3. _____

4. _____

5. _____

Now write a sentence for each compound word you formed.

6. _____

_____

7. _____

_____

8. _____

_____

_____

9. _____

_____

10. _____

_____

WORK WITH CONTRACTIONS

A *contraction* blends two words into one by replacing one or more letters with an apostrophe ('). For example:

it + is = *it's*   she + would = *she'd*

In each sentence, find the contraction. Underline it. Then write the two separate words that formed the contraction. The first one has been done for you.

1. He wonders what's keeping Sally.   _____what is_____

2. We're going to Canada for a vacation.   _____

3. She might've been to our old school.   _____

4. He said that it'll probably snow tonight.   _____

5. They just can't seem to untie that knot.   _____

6. You may feel cozy, but I'm freezing!   _____

7. Gee, wouldn't it be wild if cats really talked?   _____

8. Well, you needn't be so snippy about it!   _____

9. People say she'd be better off on her own.   _____

10. Eric, you'd better walk the dog before school.   _____

11. I promise I won't peek until you say so.   _____

12. Okay, let's have Granny's brownies now.   _____

EXPLAIN PREFIXES

Use your understanding of prefixes to complete each sentence.
The first one has been done for you.

1. A **dishonest** person would probably __not tell the truth__ .

2. If you **repay** a loan, then you _____ .

3. An **unfamiliar** language has words you _____ .

4. It's time to **defrost** the freezer when it gets _____ .

5. You might **rethink** your plans if _____ .

6. A jury that **prejudges** decides _____ .

7. If I **disinvite** Leo to my party, he _____ .

8. When you **reheat** the soup, you _____ .

9. An **impolite** person might _____ .

10. To **disconnect** the phone, just _____ .

11. When you **retrace** your steps, you go _____ .

12. The story is **incomplete**, so it is _____ .

13. If you have an **unwanted** car, you might _____ .

14. If you wear **nonskid** shoes, you probably _____ .

Name ....

EXPLAIN SUFFIXES

Use your understanding of suffixes to complete each sentence.
The first one has been done for you.

1. A **painless** experience would be _____without pain_____ .

2. A **powerful** storm would be _____ .

3. Behavior that is **childish** is _____ .

4. If you see a **lifelike** painting, you may think it is _____ .

5. Someone known for **kindness** is probably _____ .

6. You would find the **northernmost** star _____ .

7. If the stew is **salty**, it has _____ .

8. You eat **quickly** if you _____ .

9. **Friendship** describes the condition of being _____ .

10. **Adulthood** is the time when you will be _____ .

11. An **enjoyable** story is one that you _____ .

12. A **flexible** drinking straw is one that you can _____ .

13. The **fearful** kitten acted as if she felt _____ .

14. A knight who shows **loyalty** is known to be _____ .

Name ....

FIND CAPITALIZATION ERRORS

Read each sentence. Notice the three underlined words. If you see an error in capitalization, mark the letter beneath the word that has the error. If all the underlined words are capitalized correctly, choose *No Error*.

1. At a <u>Museum</u> in <u>Philadelphia</u>, you can walk in a model human <u>heart</u>. *No Error*
          (A)   (B)   (C)

2. Do you <u>know</u> what time your <u>Mother</u> is getting to <u>Kansas City</u>?   *No Error*
          (A)   (B)   (C)

3. My favorite <u>basketball</u> team used to be the <u>Chicago</u> <u>bulls</u>.   *No Error*
              (A)   (B) (C)

4. Lake <u>Erie</u> forms part of the long border between the <u>U.S.</u> and <u>Canada</u>. *No Error*
        (A)   (B)   (C)

5. <u>The</u> very first <u>Earth</u> Day was celebrated on <u>april</u> 22, 1970.   *No Error*
    (A)   (B)   (C)

6. More than 700 <u>million</u> people practice the <u>hindu</u> <u>faith</u>.   *No Error*
               (A)   (B) (C)

7. Do <u>you</u> know who was <u>President</u> of IBM in the <u>year</u> you were born? *No Error*
       (A)   (B)   (C)

8. I baby-sit for my <u>cousin</u> <u>Jake</u> every <u>thursday</u> after school.   *No Error*
              (A) (B)   (C)

9. <u>Alaska</u> is the largest state, but <u>new</u> <u>York</u> has the largest city!   *No Error*
    (A)   (B) (C)

10. <u>North</u> <u>Carolina</u> has exactly one hundred <u>Counties</u> in it.   *No Error*
     (A)   (B)   (C)

11. Do you think there is a <u>Main</u> <u>Street</u> in every small town in <u>America</u>? *No Error*
                    (A) (B)   (C)

12. The <u>declaration</u> of <u>Independence</u> was signed on the 4th day of <u>July</u>. *No Error*
      (A)   (B)   (C)

Name ....

USE CAPITAL LETTERS

Each sentence has three words that are missing their first letter.
One of these missing letters should be capitalized. Fill in the first letter of
each word so that the sentence makes sense. The first one has been
done for you.

1. __P__lease call the __d__entist to make an appointment for a __c__ heck-up.

2. The teacher said, "___pen your ___ooks to page ___hirteen."

3. My ___ittle sister loves to watch ___*eauty and the Beast* on ___ideo.

4. ___obert likes the taste of mint ___oothpaste better than the

taste of ___innamon.

5. Look through a ___elescope tonight to get a good look at the ___lanet

___ercury.

6. Visitors to the Washington ___onument can take the ___levator to the

very ___op.

7. She began the ___etter with "___ear Granny," and ___nded it with

a smiley face.

8. Martin Luther ___ing, Jr. was a great ___peaker whose words we

___emember today.

9. The New York ___ankees are one of the most famous ___aseball

teams of ___ll.

10. ___hat time do you think the ___arty will be ___ver?

11. Franny is ___earning to play "___merica" on the ___iano.

12. National ___lections next ___ear will be held on ___uesday,

November 3.

Name ....

END MARKS

Write the end mark that best completes each sentence.
Use **.** or **?** or **!** .

1. Which teams are playing at the stadium tonight

2. Oh no, I can't find my house key

3. Let's meet near the bike rack behind the school

4. Do you want to go swimming later

5. Put down those matches right this minute

6. Why is the alarm ringing at this hour

7. It has been so crowded at the museum lately

8. Hey, stop trying to read my secret diary

9. What kind of plants do you think would grow in our yard

10. Happy birthday

11. When Jenny is nervous, she twirls her hair

12. Are you bringing the potato salad or the lemonade

Name ....

USE THE END MARK

Write a sentence that fits each end mark you see.

1. **?** _____

_____

_____

2. **?** _____

_____

_____

3. **!** _____

_____

_____

4. **!** _____

_____

_____

5. **.** _____

_____

_____

6. **.** _____

_____

_____

WATCH THE PUNCTUATION

Shade the box by the sentence that has NO punctuation mistake.

1. [A] They cant read Spanish, but they can speak it.

[B] He won't be able to stay for supper.

[C] Mrs. Lopez could'nt make it to the meeting.

2. [A] The kittens were born on January 9 1999.

[B] The mama cat protected her newborns carefully

[C] We've never seen such adorable babies!

3. [A] Chicago, is the home of the deep-dish pizza pie.

[B] Kansas City is famous; for barbecued ribs.

[C] Maryland is known for its Chesapeake Bay seafood.

4. [A] Maybe we should put it in a bigger envelope.

[B] How late is the post office open tonight.

[C] Do you have? any more stamps.

5. [A] The main ingredients are flour, butter eggs, and milk.

[B] Jared likes his pizza with peppers, pineapple, and garlic.

[C] The pool is open late, on Monday Wednesday and Friday.

6. [A] The play should be over by 830 P.M.

[B] The actors must be ready by 6:00 P.M.

[C] The box office begins selling tickets at 1;30 P.M.

7. [A] I wonder how the Porcupine River in Arkansas got its name.

[B] Four past presidents have their faces carved into Mt Rushmore.

[C] E B White wrote *Charlotte's Web*.

8. [A] Larrys paintings are colorful and wild.

[B] The frame's he makes are made of natural twigs.

[C] The museum shop sells copies of famous artists' works.

Name ....

FIX PUNCTUATION ERRORS

Each sentence below is missing one or more punctuation marks.
Rewrite the sentences, adding end marks, commas, quotation marks,
or apostrophes.

1. Do you want to set up a clubhouse
Fred asked Wayne.

_____

_____

2. Fred pointed to the old tool shed the
one that nobody used anymore.

_____

3. We could paint it add rugs and pillows and hang out there said Fred.

_____

4. So the boys began to clean out the shed which took several long dusty days.

_____

5. Yuck yelled Wayne as he walked through sticky cobwebs

_____

6. After a few weeks they barely recognized that old shed

_____

7. Freds aunt gave them a rug Waynes mom gave them some old pillows.

_____

8. They painted the door to say F & W Club Private Stay Out

_____

9. Its amazing how those boys turned that old shed into a perfect hideaway.

_____

10. Now all we need is room service joked Wayne.

_____

PART 2:

WRITING STYLES

Name ....

CONTINUE A SENTENCE

Finish each sentence. Then write another sentence that continues the thought.

1. That dessert was way too _____

_____

_____

2. When I heard the helicopters overhead _____

_____

_____

3. The train slowly entered _____

_____

_____

4. The radio was playing some _____

_____

_____

5. He stormed into his room and _____

_____

_____

6. I've always wanted to _____

_____

_____

WRITE COMPLETE SENTENCES

Turn each phrase into a complete sentence. Write it on the spaces given.

1. that she tried to read _____

_____

2. when we left the stadium _____

_____

3. waited around for hours _____

_____

4. if we are allowed to _____

_____

5. beneath a pile of newspapers _____

_____

6. with no real plan in mind _____

_____

7. immediately grabbed the phone _____

_____

8. as the light began to fade _____

_____

COMBINE TWO SENTENCES

Read each pair of short sentences. Combine both ideas into one longer sentence. Write the combined sentence using words from the box to join ideas.

and	because	but	for	neither	or	since
although	if	until	while	so	when	such as

1. The coach blows her whistle. The game stops.

_____

_____

2. Gina loves hip-hop music. Tony prefers salsa.

_____

_____

3. Arbor Day is in June. Labor Day is in September.

_____

_____

4. I selected a purple bedspread. Purple is my favorite color.

_____

_____

5. The traffic stops. The crossing guard escorts the children.

_____

_____

6. Abby enjoys writing poetry. Limericks are poems.

_____

_____

FIX RUN-ON SENTENCES

Fix each run-on sentence by separating it into two sentences. Cross out unneeded words. Add the necessary punctuation and capitalization.

1. Many modern businesses have Web sites customers can visit the Web sites any hour of the day or night.

2. The first Web sites were pretty dull and hard to use people who found their way to them weren't so sure what to do when they got there.

3. Now there are Web sites for just about any subject you can imagine there are even Web sites that just list other Web sites!

4. People argue over whether there should be separate Web sites for children and for adults some people think this is a good idea but others aren't so sure.

5. Families can add software to their computers to stop children from visiting Web sites that parents don't approve of this software is easy to use and not expensive to buy.

6. I like Web sites where I can learn cool facts of the day I also like to browse Web sites about famous people I admire.

7. Our family is creating a Web site where we can post family pictures and have online reunions our cousins in Japan are working on the same idea.

8. Instant messaging (IM) is very popular today people of older generations can't believe how much time young people today spend using IM.

9. The wildest IM experience I ever had was when we set up a four-way chat Mom and I were at home in New Jersey my dad was in Mexico my granddad was in England and my aunt and uncle were in Hawaii!

10. It's hard for me to imagine a world without computers but my grand-parents can they always remind me that they grew up without a television.

AVOID DOUBLE NEGATIVES

Each sentence below incorrectly uses double negatives.
Rewrite the sentence to make it correct.

1. They won't ask no questions.

_____

_____

2. She don't never eat liver.

_____

_____

3. We hardly had no time to rest.

_____

_____

4. There ain't nobody at the door.

_____

_____

5. You can't get no help from them.

_____

_____

6. I never saw no shooting stars.

_____

_____

FIGURE OUT THE ERROR

Each sentence below contains one kind of error—or no error at all. Choose the best answer.

1. So, are you sure you know all your times tables.

- [A] capitalization error
- [B] spelling error
- [C] punctuation error
- [D] no error

2. Which is the top number in a fraction—the numerator or the denominator?

- [A] capitalization error
- [B] spelling error
- [C] punctuation error
- [D] no error

3. Geometry, the study of lines angles and shapes is my favorite topic in math.

- [A] capitalization error
- [B] spelling error
- [C] punctuation error
- [D] no error

4. Our math teacher told us why the equil sign is made of two lines.

- [A] capitalization error
- [B] spelling error
- [C] punctuation error
- [D] no error

5. Our Principal says that he is more than two yards tall.

- [A] capitalization error
- [B] spelling error
- [C] punctuation error
- [D] no error

6. My ruller is marked in inches along one edge and in centimeters along the other.

- [A] capitalization error
- [B] spelling error
- [C] punctuation error
- [D] no error

7. We won't study percents until next year, but I know what it means to get 100% on a test!

- [A] capitalization error
- [B] spelling error
- [C] punctuation error
- [D] no error

8. Most Americans do not use Metric Measurements in their daily lives.

- [A] capitalization error
- [B] spelling error
- [C] punctuation error
- [D] no error

Name ....

CHOOSE THE SYNONYM

Read the sentence. Pick the word that is closest in meaning to the underlined word.

1. They felt so <u>drowsy</u> after the holiday banquet.

　A full　　　B energetic　　C relaxed　　D sleepy

2. You can <u>obtain</u> samples at the customer service window.

　A get　　　B purchase　　C borrow　　D copy

3. Emergency workers responded to <u>urgent</u> calls for help.

　A casual　　B critical　　C noisy　　D minor

4. We'd like to <u>extend</u> our vacation by several days.

　A limit　　　B cancel　　C continue　　D remember

5. People who work <u>hastily</u> are more likely to make sloppy mistakes.

　A speedily　B darkly　　C casually　　D fearfully

6. When Judy gets upset, her lips tend to <u>quiver</u>.

　A tighten　B hurt　　C tremble　　D droop

7. The new student looked around the room with <u>envy</u> over all he had missed.

　A jealousy　B anger　　C awe　　D pleasure

8. What is that annoying <u>clatter</u> coming from the attic?

　A odor　　B conversation　C gossip　　D racket

9. The patient shows <u>gradual</u> improvement with each passing day.

　A rapid　　B surprising　　C step-by-step　D no

10. The helper seemed too <u>juvenile</u> to take her duties seriously.

　A immature　B weary　　C reckless　　D healthy

CHOOSE THE ANTONYM

Read the sentence. Pick the word that means the opposite of the underlined word.

1. The mayor's <u>loyal</u> aide takes care of every assignment.
   A unfaithful   C part-time
   B professional   D reliable

2. He is careful never to make <u>shallow</u> remarks, especially about key issues.
   A confusing   C deep
   B thoughtless   D supporting

3. "The mayor's most <u>precious</u> possession is her fine reputation," the aide says.
   A valuable   B ordinary   C expensive   D unusual

4. In the upcoming election, it isn't clear which candidate will <u>triumph</u>.
   A transfer   B vote   C win   D lose

5. Some reporters try to <u>expose</u> a candidate's weaknesses.
   A disguise   B reveal   C research   D interrupt

6. But this <u>vibrant</u> mayor has many followers.
   A lucky   B energetic   C lifeless   D intelligent

7. In last night's speech, the mayor emphasized two <u>valid</u> reasons to support her.
   A sound   B unconvincing   C important   D roundabout

8. The first was about public service, to which she claims <u>devotion</u>.
   A commitment   B neglect   C uncertainty   D attraction

9. The second was her success in cleaning up <u>toxic</u> waste from the region.
   A harmful   B filthy   C harmless   D cluttered

10. Her trusty aide was there to <u>magnify</u> all the successes of her term in office.
    A boost   B stress   C repeat   D lessen

USE FIGURES OF SPEECH

Mark the answer that has the same meaning as the expression in **boldface.**

1. Don't **beat around the bush** anymore.
- A avoid the main point
- B rake the leaves
- C repeat yourself
- D get frustrated

2. Let's wait until all this **blows over**.
- A comes apart
- B gets worse
- C exhales
- D passes

3. It's an enjoyable way to **break the ice**.
- A climb a mountain
- B relax and interact
- C chill the room
- D stop the arguing

4. We must never **cut corners** on safety.
- A be foolish
- B disagree
- C take shortcuts
- D get excited

5. Dan got **cold feet** at the last minute.
- A became brave
- B wore heavy socks
- C lost his nerve
- D stepped in a puddle

6. I'm totally ready to **hit the hay**.
- A go to bed
- B be a farmer
- C do my exercises
- D take a break

7. He's sick of playing **second fiddle**.
- A practicing country music
- B counting his blessings
- C hurrying
- D being the next best

8. That attitude makes them **see red**!
- A feel embarrassed
- B get angry
- C want to read
- D blush

9. Okay, it's time to **throw in the towel**.
- A do the laundry
- B give up
- C calm down
- D ask for seconds

10. That movie was really **for the birds**.
- A about nature
- B breezy and light
- C terrible
- D scary

Name ....

EXPLAIN FIGURES OF SPEECH

Each sentence has a figure of speech in **boldface**. Think about what the words mean. Rewrite each sentence in your own words. Keep the same meaning without using the figure of speech.

1. When my parents saw the damage, they really **flew off the handle**.

_____

_____

2. The theater usher was **pulling my leg** when he said to fasten my

seat belt.

_____

_____

3. That new suit **fits like a glove**.

_____

_____

4. I'd really like to join you, but can I **take a rain check** until later?

_____

_____

5. Dad was sorry, but he said it would **cost an arm and a leg**.

_____

_____

6. She was feeling slightly **under the weather** last night.

_____

_____

ADD SUPPORTING DETAILS

Read each sentence. Then write two more sentences that add supporting details.

1. It started out like any other school day at the bus stop.

_____

_____

_____

_____

2. The artist was preparing to start her latest painting.

_____

_____

_____

_____

3. The roller coaster moved slowly up the steep slope.

_____

_____

_____

_____

4. Each summer, the town holds an all-day July 4th festival.

_____

_____

_____

TOPIC SENTENCE AND SUPPORT

Read each topic sentence. Then read the three sentences that follow it. Circle the letter next to the sentence that best supports the topic sentence.

1. Topic sentence: A gas well in Oklahoma is the deepest well in America.
  a. Natural gas is used for heating and cooking in homes and businesses.
  b. The well goes down 31,441 feet into the earth—nearly six miles!
  c. Oklahoma became a state in 1907.

2. Topic sentence: The community of Climax, Colorado, holds an unusual record.
  a. It is located west of the capital city of Denver.
  b. Mining has been important to the area for nearly a century.
  c. Perched at 11,360 feet above sea level, it's the highest settlement in America.

3. Topic sentence: Yellowstone is the oldest national park in the world.
  a. President Grant established it on March 1, 1872.
  b. It includes parts of Wyoming, Montana, and Idaho.
  c. Wildfires there in 1988 burned over a million acres of land.

4. Topic sentence: Mt. Waialeale in Hawaii is the wettest place on Earth!
  a. It is located on the small island of Kauai.
  b. This soggy spot gets about 480 inches of rain every year.
  c. In the Hawaiian language, the word *waialeale* means "rippling water."

5. Topic sentence: The exact geographic center of Connecticut is in Hartford.
  a. Perhaps this is one reason why Hartford is the state capital.
  b. Connecticut is one of the New England states.
  c. The city of Hartford has a population of about 122,000 people.

6. Topic sentence: The United States and Canada share a long and friendly border.
  a. Canada, to our north, is America's largest neighbor.
  b. The border between Mexico and the United States is about 1,933 miles long.
  c. The U.S.-Canada border runs a total length of about 5,525 miles.

UNITY IN PARAGRAPHS

Read each paragraph to find the main idea. Underline its topic sentence. Cross out one sentence that does NOT belong.

1. Can you imagine a world without bridges? Bridges let travelers cross water, roads, rails, and deep pits safely. The oldest bridges were probably tree trunks put across streams. Later, people made simple bridges out of rope, timber, and stone. Someone filmed the collapse of the Tacoma Narrows Bridge in 1940. Modern bridges are made mostly of concrete and steel.

2. Picture the bridges you have seen or crossed. Bridges can be truly beautiful and graceful. Some bridges have lovely arches of stone or cable. Others have pleasing structures that provide support and good design. Hard stone, such as granite, might be used to build a bridge.

3. Nature itself has sometimes been a fine bridge builder. Sometimes stepping stones seem to be perfectly placed in a shallow stream, as if expecting hikers to cross at any moment. Natural bridges exist where giant stones arch over an open space. Natural Bridges National Monument is in Utah. Tree branches sometimes fall just right to offer a simple walkway across a ditch.

4. Some bridges need to move so that boats can pass beneath them. Three types of moveable bridges are lift bridges, swing bridges, and drawbridges. Lift bridges have a middle section that lifts up so boats can pass under, and then moves back into place so traffic can continue. Swing bridges rotate to form an opening, and then swing back into place. Another name for a drawbridge is a *bascule*. Drawbridges open up in the middle, with each half lifting to form a wide open space.

USE SIGNAL WORDS

To link ideas together smoothly, writers use signal words and phrases. Mark the best signal word or phrase to fit each sentence.

1. It was the annual barbecue, _____ our entire family gathers for a picnic.

- A with
- C because
- B although
- D when

2. We always gather for this all-day party on the third Sunday in July, _____ what the weather may bring.

- A despite
- C likewise
- B because of
- D during

3. The kids usually play _____ the adults prepare the food and visit.

- A like
- C while
- B during
- D since

4. Some of the older folks entertain by playing instruments, _____ the younger ones usually bring their own CDs.

- A thus
- C although
- B since
- D already

5. My favorite thing is the family tug-of-war, _____ one team is made up of everyone under 35, and the other team is made up of everyone over 35.

- A in which
- C unless
- B against
- D instead of

6. We always take group photos; _____ who'd believe that we were all there?

- A otherwise
- C now
- B and
- D while

7. I usually don't eat meat, _____ that steak looked too good to resist.

- A like
- C therefore
- B but
- D since

8. There were pies of all kinds— _____ apple, peach, lemon, cherry, and berry.

- A unlike
- C likewise
- B then
- D namely

PART 3:
THE
WRITING
PROCESS

Name ....

PREWRITING: TAKE NOTES

The doctor calls your house to speak with your mom. Since your mom is not home, you have to take notes about the phone call.

Complete the form to leave Mom a message.
(You can make up information that fits this situation.)

MESSAGE FOR: _____

TIME OF CALL: _____

DATE: _____

NAME OF CALLER: _____

WHO IS THIS PERSON? _____

MESSAGE: _____

_____

_____

_____

_____

_____

HOW TO RESPOND: _____

CALLER'S PHONE NUMBER: _____

WHO TOOK THIS MESSAGE? _____

PREWRITING: NARROW A TOPIC

If your topic is too broad, it will be hard for you to treat it well. Examine this example of narrowing a topic:

BROAD TOPIC: Movies

NARROW TOPIC: Adventure movies

NARROWER TOPIC: Movies about adventures in space

Complete the chart by narrowing the given topics.

BROAD	NARROW	NARROWER
1. team sports	indoor team sports	
2. foods	desserts	
3. ocean creatures	sharks	
4. instruments		playing the harp
5. South America	jungles of South America	
6. lakes	The Great Lakes	
7. careers	careers in medicine	
8. transportation	one-person vehicles	
9. planets		Is there life on Mars?
10. dinosaurs	meat-eating dinosaurs	

Name ....

PREWRITING: USE STORY BLOCKS

Plan a story for each title below. Fill in the blocks with your ideas for the story's setting, as well as the beginning, middle, and end.

Lost in the Woods!

Setting:		
Beginning	**Middle**	**End**

In the Old Trunk

Setting:		
Beginning	**Middle**	**End**

Name ....

PREWRITING: USE A CHARACTER MAP

Develop a character for a story. Use this character map to figure out what this character is like.

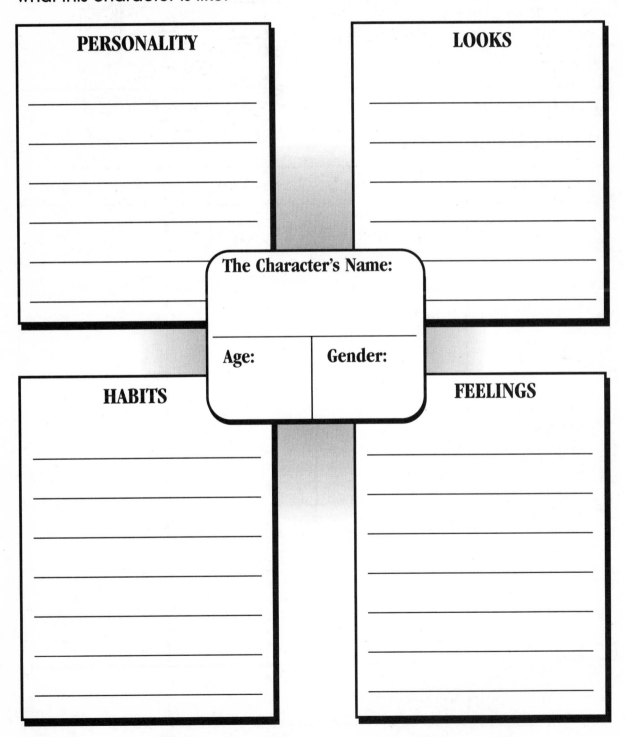

PERSONALITY

LOOKS

The Character's Name:

Age: **Gender:**

HABITS

FEELINGS

Name ....

You can use a chart to gather details before you write. Later, you can use the words to express your ideas vividly. Complete the chart for a whale watch off Cape Cod.

Watching for Whales in the Atlantic Ocean

Emotion Words	Five-Senses Words	Setting Details	People Details
curious	salty smell mist on glasses	choppy sea	crusty captain

PREWRITING: I KNOW, I WANT TO KNOW

Look at each picture. Write some facts you know about it. Write some ideas you'd like to know about it.

	I KNOW...	I WANT TO KNOW...
1.		
2.		
3.		
4.		
5.		

Name ....

PREWRITING: PLAN QUESTIONS

You can gather information by asking good questions. An EMT (emergency medical technician) works in an ambulance, helping people in trouble. Imagine an EMT visits your class. Write some good questions to ask.

1. What _____

_____

_____ ?

2. Who _____

_____

_____ ?

3. How _____

_____

_____ ?

4. When _____

_____

_____ ?

5. Why _____

_____

_____ ?

6. Where _____

_____

_____ ?

7. Which _____

_____

_____ ?

Name ....

PREWRITING: RESPONSE TO READING

Use a chart to plan a book report. The ideas you list can help you write your report fully and thoughtfully. Pick a book you have read or are reading now. Then list ideas or questions in each category given.

BOOK TITLE: _____

AUTHOR: _____

SETTING: _____

_____

_____

CHARACTERS: _____

_____

_____

PLOT: _____

_____

_____

THEME: _____

_____

_____

WRITER'S STYLE: _____

_____

_____

LINKS (similarities to other works): _____

_____

_____

PREWRITING: FACT vs. OPINION

When you gather details, you must be able to tell facts from opinions. Each statement below is about cameras. Is the statement *fact* or *opinion*? Write F or O on the line next to each statement.

_____ **1.** Cameras bring happiness and pleasure.

_____ **2.** Joseph Niépce of France took the first photograph in 1827.

_____ **3.** He tried to photograph the view from his window.

_____ **4.** The quality of that first picture wasn't worth the hours he spent on it.

_____ **5.** But Niépce was the best photographer of his day.

_____ **6.** Niépce took on a young partner named Louis Daguerre.

_____ **7.** By 1837, Daguerre figured out how to make photos in far less time.

_____ **8.** Early photographs cost too much and were too hard to make.

_____ **9.** 1888 was the most important year in camera history.

_____ **10.** That's when George Eastman invented a simple camera that used film.

_____ **11.** Nowadays, everyone loves to take pictures.

_____ **12.** Almost anyone can learn to use a camera.

_____ **13.** Digital cameras are much better than film cameras.

_____ **14.** Being a photographer is one of the best jobs you could have.

PREWRITING: LIBRARY RESOURCES (1)

Mark the best answer to each question about library materials.

1. In which section of the library would you find a book about rockets?
- [A] fiction
- [B] biography
- [C] nonfiction
- [D] sports

2. Which book would give information about Egyptian painting?
- [A] an atlas
- [B] a book on deserts
- [C] an art book
- [D] a dictionary

3. If you know the name of a book you want to borrow, which part of the card catalog should you check?
- [A] subject card
- [B] index card
- [C] author card
- [D] title card

4. You want to know who won the first World Cup Soccer tournament. Which resource would you choose?
- [A] an encyclopedia
- [B] an almanac
- [C] a soccer Web site
- [D] an interview with a soccer coach

5. To know if a book on submarines tells of the sinking of the *Kursk*, check
- [A] Chapter 7.
- [B] the index.
- [C] the book jacket.
- [D] a review.

6. Every book tells the year in which it was published. This fact is called
- [A] the spine.
- [B] the dedication.
- [C] the call number.
- [D] the copyright date.

7. Where in a book will you find the name of its author?
- [A] in the glossary
- [B] in the index
- [C] on the title page
- [D] in the table of contents

8. To find the capital of Kenya, which resource would you check?
- [A] an almanac
- [B] an encyclopedia
- [C] an atlas
- [D] all of the above

PREWRITING: LIBRARY RESOURCES (2)

Mark the best answer to each question.

1. Sadie wants to know about Sir Arthur Conan Doyle. In which volume of the encyclopedia should she look?

- A A
- B C
- C D
- D S

2. Al is writing a report on passenger helicopters. Which book probably won't help?

- A *Into Deep Space*
- B *Modern Aircraft*
- C *The 'Copter Chronicles*
- D *Heliports and Helipads*

3. Penny wants to see a map of Easter Island. Which is the best source for her to check?

- A an atlas
- B a thesaurus
- C a dictionary
- D a holiday magazine

4. Gabe wants to find the definition of the word *dulcet*. To which part of the dictionary should he turn?

- A the beginning
- B the middle
- C the end
- D cannot tell

5. Rasheed wants to know the meaning of *parody*. It will be on the dictionary page that has which guide words?

- A parrot / partial
- B parlor / parole
- C parent / parochial
- D parallel / pardon

6. Jen wants to see pictures of ancient rock art. Which might be the best place for her to look?

- A a rock video
- B a filmstrip about ancestors
- C a CD-ROM on caves
- D a Web site on Alaska

7. To learn the symptoms of a skin condition called *psoriasis*, which of these sources probably won't help?

- A a thesaurus
- B a medical dictionary
- C a home health-care book
- D an interview with a doctor

8. You want to know which albums won Grammy awards in 2002. Which resource would be your best choice?

- A an almanac
- B a music Web site
- C an encyclopedia
- D an interview with a guitarist

Name ....

DRAFTING: WRITE THE STEPS

Imagine someone who has never seen a pencil or a pencil
sharpener! Give that person step-by-step written instructions for when
and how to sharpen a pencil. Give all details clearly and in order.
Use as many steps as you need.

1. _____

_____

_____

_____

_____

2. _____

_____

_____

_____

_____

3. _____

_____

_____

_____

4. _____

_____

_____

_____

5. _____

_____

_____

6. _____

_____

_____

7. _____

_____

_____

8. _____

_____

_____

Name ....

DRAFTING: ORGANIZE THE SENTENCES

Read the four topics in the box below. Then read the sentences that follow.
Write A, B, C, or D to match each sentence with the topic it supports.

A. Adopting a Pet
B. How to Make an Igloo
C. At the Carnival
D. A Hot-Air Balloon Ride

_____ **1.** The air smelled like cotton candy and caramel apples.

_____ **2.** The take-off was set for just after sunrise on Saturday morning.

_____ **3.** This structure is fairly easy to make and surprisingly warm.

_____ **4.** It's always best to know the animal's previous owner.

_____ **5.** People are forced to give away cats and dogs for many reasons.

_____ **6.** Native peoples built shelters with whatever was plentiful—snow!

_____ **7.** Most people hurry to the rides, but we went straight for the food.

_____ **8.** The basket can safely hold three or four people, plus the pilot.

_____ **9.** Before take-off, passengers must read a list of important safety rules.

_____ **10.** At the admission booth, the clerks were selling ticket books for $10.

_____ **11.** The most important tool is a sharp knife with a long, thin blade.

_____ **12.** Be prepared to accept the animal as it is, and show patience and love.

_____ **13.** It's always a good idea to take your new family member to see a vet.

_____ **14.** The only sound we heard was the _whoosh_ of the burner heating the air.

_____ **15.** We won a huge stuffed animal, two live goldfish, and a baseball cap.

_____ **16.** It should be just big enough for the people and animals to fit inside.

Name ....

DRAFTING: TOPIC SENTENCES

Write a strong topic sentence that pulls together each group
of sentences.

1. The bright hallways smelled of fresh paint.
The bulletin boards were decorated with cheery welcome signs.
Stacks of crisp new books waited in each room.

_____

_____

_____

2. People crowded along both sides of the street.
They waved flags and banners and held colorful balloons.
The distant sound of drums and horns could be heard to the north.

_____

_____

_____

3. We wore our most comfortable shoes for the day.
We hoped to raise money for a worthy cause.
Reporters and photographers were there to cover the event.
Free water stops were set up every few blocks.

_____

_____

_____

4. The cool air smelled salty and damp.
We pulled our rain gear up over our heads and climbed aboard.
Seagulls squawked and flew overhead as we pulled away from the dock.

_____

_____

_____

Name ....

DRAFTING: KNOW YOUR AUDIENCE

Select a topic you know a lot about. Write TWO different paragraphs about it. Write the first paragraph for people who know as much about the topic as you do. Write the second paragraph for people who know little or nothing about it.

TOPIC: _____

1. Paragraph for an Informed Audience

_____

_____

_____

_____

_____

_____

_____

_____

2. Paragraph for an Uninformed Audience

_____

_____

_____

_____

_____

_____

_____

_____

DRAFTING: KNOW YOUR PURPOSE

Your purpose for writing should guide how you write.
Read the example below. It shows two sentences on the same topic.
But each was written for a different purpose.

TOPIC: A child in a robot costume

PURPOSE: To amuse	PURPOSE: To frighten
A kid dressed in boxes and tin cans clanked up our front steps.	A terrifying Frankenstein-like creature slowly crept up to our doorbell.

Write two sentences on each topic. Make each sentence serve a different purpose.

1. TOPIC: A dancer's performance

PURPOSE: To praise _____

_____

PURPOSE: To criticize _____

_____

_____

2. TOPIC: Soaring in a hang-glider

PURPOSE: To thrill _____

_____

PURPOSE: To caution against _____

_____

3. TOPIC: Mom's new outfit

PURPOSE: To flatter _____

_____

PURPOSE: To hide your dislike _____

_____

EDITING: CHOOSE THE BEST SENTENCE

Choose the sentence in each group that is written best.

1. A Alan is teaching his puppy to be rolling over.
   B Alan is teaching his puppy to roll over.
   C Alan's puppy is teaching to roll him over.

2. A The moon looks like a silver fingernail in the sky.
   B Like a silver fingernail in the sky, the silver moon looks.
   C The moon looking like a silver fingernail in the sky.

3. A Have you seen those fold-up wheels with inline skates?
   B Have you seen those inline skates with fold-up wheels?
   C Are you seeing those inline skates with fold-up wheels?

4. A Leaving a big mess, a raccoon got into our trash, and it was last night.
   B A raccoon, last night, got into our trash, leaving a big mess.
   C A raccoon got into our trash last night, leaving a big mess.

5. A Tina wakes up each morning much earlier always than do I.
   B Tina always wakes up each morning much earlier than I do.
   C Always, each morning, Tina wakes up, but much earlier than I do.

6. A The words go by too fast for me, in that song, to understand them.
   B The words, for me to understand them, go by too fast in that song.
   C The words to that song go by too fast for me to understand them.

7. A The smell of blueberry muffins baking in the oven, do you notice?
   B Do you notice, baking in the oven, the blueberry muffins smell?
   C Do you notice the smell of blueberry muffins baking in the oven?

8. A Nobody was there today the third time today that the phone rang.
   B That's the third time today that the phone rang and nobody was there.
   C That's the third time today and nobody was there that the phone rang.

9. A Those old ice skates must be somewhere in this messy hall closet.
   B Those messy ice skates somewhere in this old hall closet must be.
   C Somewhere in this messy hall closet, but where are those old ice skates?

10. A Because it ruins tapes, something keeps being wrong with our VCR.
   B Something is wrong with our VCR because it keeps ruining tapes.
   C Something is wrong with our VCR because it keeps ruined tapes.

EDITING: REMOVE EXTRA DETAILS

Each paragraph below has a sentence that doesn't belong.
Find that sentence and cross it out.

1. I'm going to make a spaghetti dinner tonight. I know how to do everything myself. I'll use wagon wheel pasta because I like that shape. I'll add mushrooms to the sauce to make it chewy. Dad is picking up my brother and sister in time for dinner. I also have to make a salad, which is easy. The hard part is to figure out what order to do things so it will all come out together.

2. Nan just started trumpet lessons. She's terrible at it so far, but she will get better. The trumpet is a very loud instrument that can sound pretty weird, especially the way Nan plays it! She is practicing to play the same note three times in a row exactly the same way. She says that it's much harder to do than you would think. Her trumpet was made in Elkhart, Indiana.

3. The lines to get in to see the stock-car race were very long. It was the first race of the season, and last year's champion will be driving. My Uncle Arnold once drove stock cars. We waited for almost an hour to get in, but it was such a gorgeous day that nobody minded. Finally, we got great seats—and in our favorite part of the grandstand.

4. You've heard of ice hockey and field hockey, but do you know about water hockey? Actually, that would be *under*water hockey. It's a team game played at the bottom of a swimming pool! Players wear masks, fins, snorkels, and protective gear as they try to get the puck into the goal. Other water sports are rowing, swimming, and diving. But the real trick to underwater hockey is teamwork because everybody comes up for air quite often.

REVISING: FIX THE MISTAKES

Here is the first draft of a letter. It has several underlined mistakes. Find the answer choices for each underlined error. Choose the best answer to fix the mistake.

1. A October 26, 2002.
  B October 26: 2002
  C October 26, 2002

2. A Dear Mr. Devine.
  B Dear Mr. Devine,
  C Dear Mr. Devine

3. A I'm writing
  B IM writing
  C i'm writing

4. A Green Bay, Wisconsin.
  B Green Bay Wisconsin,
  C Green Bay, Wisconsin,

5. A My parents say
  B My parents' say
  C My parent say

6. A Can you send a map!
  B Can you send a Map?
  C Can you send a map?

7. A Please answer Soon.
  B Please answer soon.
  C Please Answer Soon.

8. A november,
  B November.
  C November,

(1) October 26 2002

(2) Dear Mr Devine.

Hello! **(3)** Im writing to ask you for information. I found your name in a book on woodworking. It says that your workshop in **(4)** green Bay Wisconsin is open to visitors by appointment. My scout troop is doing a woodworking project.
(5) My parent's say they will drive me to visit if you give permission. Is this true? May we visit? When are you open? **(6)** Can you send a map.
(7) please Answer soon? We hope to visit in **(8)** november hopefully before Thanksgiving. Thanks for your help.

Best regards,

Carl Bromley

REVISING: LIVEN UP DULL SENTENCES

Dull sentences can be made more vivid and lively. Here is an example:

Dull sentence: *The girl had her lunch.*
Better sentence: *The hungry girl wolfed down a taco in two huge bites.*

Make each dull sentence better. Add precise nouns and vivid verbs and adjectives.

1. The first day of vacation is so good.

_____

_____

_____

2. It's nice to get a chance to be lazy.

_____

_____

3. There will be no homework tonight. _____

_____

_____

4. I don't have to get up early unless I want to. _____

_____

_____

5. Well, it is harder to see my friends. _____

_____

_____

6. Truthfully, vacation can get boring after a while.

_____

_____

PART 4:
WRITING ACTIVITIES

> • **Exposition** is writing that informs, explains, or gives information.
>
> • **Narration** is writing that tells a story.
>
> • **Description** is writing that paints pictures using sensory details.
>
> • **Expression** is writing that conveys thoughts and feelings from one's experience.
>
> • **Persuasion** is writing that tries to convince others.
>
> • **Response to Literature** is writing that gives thoughtful reactions to literature.
>
> • **Practical Writing** is real-life writing.

Name ....

WRITING: EXPOSITION

Choose one of the following topics for writing:

- **A review of a toothpaste you like (or dislike)**
- **A letter of advice to help someone who has a quick temper**
- **A summary of the plot of a movie, TV show, book, or story**
- **An evaluation of what makes a fine teacher**
- **A set of instructions for preparing your favorite meal**

Use the steps of the writing process as you work:

1. Gather and organize your ideas and details.

2. Choose your audience and purpose.

3. Draft your composition. Use more paper as needed.

4. Edit for content and style.

5. Proofread for grammar, spelling, punctuation, and capitalization errors.

_____

_____

_____

_____

_____

_____

_____

_____

_____

_____

_____

Name ....

WRITING: NARRATION

Choose one of the following topics for writing:

- **A story about someone you will never forget**
- **A story about a funny family episode**
- **A brief tale that shows your sense of humor**
- **A story about a misunderstanding**
- **A tale of a strange experience**

Use the steps of the writing process as you work:

1. Gather and organize your ideas and details.

2. Choose your audience and purpose.

3. Draft your composition. Use more paper as needed.

4. Edit for content and style.

5. Proofread for grammar, spelling, punctuation, and capitalization errors.

_____

_____

_____

_____

_____

_____

_____

_____

_____

_____

Name ....

WRITING: DESCRIPTION

Choose one of the following topics for writing:

- **A description of a beautiful place you have visited**
- **An observation about a unique family member or friend**
- **A description of an imaginary creature**
- **A description of an important invention**
- **A memory of a dream or fantasy**

Use the steps of the writing process as you work:

1. Gather and organize your ideas and details.

2. Choose your audience and purpose.

3. Draft your composition. Use more paper as needed.

4. Edit for content and style.

5. Proofread for grammar, spelling, punctuation, and capitalization errors.

_____

_____

_____

_____

_____

_____

_____

_____

_____

_____

_____

_____

Name ....

WRITING: EXPRESSION

Choose one of the following topics for writing:

- **A time when something unexpected happened to you**
- **A journal entry about something that upset you**
- **An e-mail or letter to a friend you haven't seen or spoken to in a long time**
- **A memory of an event from your early childhood**
- **A letter describing a special souvenir or keepsake**

Use the steps of the writing process as you work:

1. Gather and organize your ideas and details.

2. Choose your audience and purpose.

3. Draft your composition. Use more paper as needed.

4. Edit for content and style.

5. Proofread for grammar, spelling, punctuation, and capitalization errors.

_____

_____

_____

_____

_____

_____

_____

_____

_____

_____

_____

Name ....

WRITING: PERSUASION

Choose one of the following topics for writing:

- **A letter to the editor of the newspaper recommending safe new bicycle paths**

- **A list of pointers to help a new student get used to your school**

- **A speech you would give if you wanted to be class president**

- **A press release advertising a sports team you like**

- **A public service announcement asking people to clean up their neighborhoods**

Use the steps of the writing process as you work:

1. Gather and organize your ideas and details.

2. Choose your audience and purpose.

3. Draft your composition. Use more paper as needed.

4. Edit for content and style.

5. Proofread for grammar, spelling, punctuation, and capitalization errors.

_____

_____

_____

_____

_____

_____

_____

_____

_____

Name ....

WRITING: RESPONSE TO LITERATURE

Choose one of the following topics for writing:

- **Advice to a character in a book, play, poem, or short story**
- **A letter to an author or illustrator of a book you liked (or disliked)**
- **A review of a book, story, play, or poem for the school newsletter**
- **A critical review of a movie you did not enjoy**
- **A "blurb" to go on a book jacket to get readers' attention**

Use the steps of the writing process as you work:

1. Gather and organize your ideas and details.

2. Choose your audience and purpose.

3. Draft your composition. Use more paper as needed.

4. Edit for content and style.

5. Proofread for grammar, spelling, punctuation, and capitalization errors.

_____

_____

_____

_____

_____

_____

_____

_____

_____

_____

Name ....

WRITING: PRACTICAL WRITING

Choose one of the following topics for writing:

- **A classified ad for selling your old computer**
- **A letter to a pet shop, offering to work there on Saturdays**
- **A poster explaining the rules of the school lunch room**
- **An invitation to a costume party**
- **A message you might record on your home telephone answering machine**

Use the steps of the writing process as you work:

1. Gather and organize your ideas and details.

2. Choose your audience and purpose.

3. Draft your composition. Use more paper as needed.

4. Edit for content and style.

5. Proofread for grammar, spelling, punctuation, and capitalization errors.

_____

_____

_____

_____

_____

_____

_____

_____

_____

_____

BUBBLE PRACTICE SHEET

Write your name in the boxes below, then fill in the bubble for each letter.

FIRST NAME

Ⓐ Ⓑ Ⓒ Ⓓ Ⓔ Ⓕ Ⓖ Ⓗ Ⓘ Ⓙ Ⓚ Ⓛ Ⓜ Ⓝ Ⓞ Ⓟ Ⓠ Ⓡ Ⓢ Ⓣ Ⓤ Ⓥ Ⓦ Ⓧ Ⓨ Ⓩ

LAST NAME

Ⓐ Ⓑ Ⓒ Ⓓ Ⓔ Ⓕ Ⓖ Ⓗ Ⓘ Ⓙ Ⓚ Ⓛ Ⓜ Ⓝ Ⓞ Ⓟ Ⓠ Ⓡ Ⓢ Ⓣ Ⓤ Ⓥ Ⓦ Ⓧ Ⓨ Ⓩ

WRITER'S SELF-EVALUATION CHECKLIST

Refer to this checklist to help you improve your writing.

❏ Have you written for your intended audience?

❏ Does your introduction grab readers?

❏ Did you get across your main ideas?

❏ Have you stuck to your topic?

❏ Do you offer enough details, descriptions, facts, or other information?

❏ Have you cut out unnecessary details?

❏ Is your point of view consistent throughout?

❏ Have you used complete sentences?

❏ Is your piece presented in sensible or logical order?

❏ Have you used transitions to help your piece flow smoothly?

❏ Have you varied sentence style and length?

❏ Does your conclusion work?

❏ Do your characters make sense? Do they speak and act as you wish them to?

❏ Have you described the setting?

❏ Have you included sensory details?

❏ Have you substituted vivid verbs, exciting adjectives, and other precise words?

❏ Have you indented new paragraphs?

❏ Have you proofread for grammar, spelling, capitalization, and punctuation?

❏ Is your handwriting neat and clear?

TEACHER NOTES and SELECTED ANSWERS

Part 1: Conventions of Grammar and Mechanics

Find the Noun (p. 8)
1. C 2. B 3. D 4. B 5. B 6. D 7. B 8. A 9. B
10. C 11. B 12. B 13. D 14. D

Noun Names (p. 9)
1. thing 2. persons 3. thing 4. place 5. thing
6. idea 7. person 8. idea 9. thing 10. thing or idea
11. persons 12. place

Write the Plural (p. 10)
2. workers 3. tables 4. branches 5. boxes
6. ponies 7. ladies 8. monkeys 9. cliffs
10. shelves 11. lives 12. heroes 13. radios
14. mice 15. oxen 16. sheep

Write the Singular (p. 11)
2. stage 3. inch 4. wish 5. tax 6. country
7. cherry 8. journey 9. elf 10. loaf 11. echo
12. zero 13. auto 14. man 15. deer

Finish the Sentence (p. 12)
2. man 3. bus 4. wishes 5. wolves 6. solo
7. potato 8. key 9. teeth 10. moose

Common Nouns, Proper Nouns (p. 13)
Answers will vary.

Identify Kinds of Nouns (p. 14)
1. B 2. A 3. A 4. C 5. B 6. D 7. A 8. A 9. A
10. A 11. B 12. D 13. C 14. D 15. A 16. C
17. C 18. A 19. B 20. A

Pick the Best Noun (p. 15)
1. d 2. a 3. b 4. c 5. b 6. c 7. b 8. d 9. a 10. b

Pick the Pronoun (p. 16)
1. b 2. c 3. d 4. c 5. d 6. d 7. b 8. d 9. a 10. d

Pronouns and Antecedents (p. 17)
1. C 2. A 3. B 4. C 5. B 6. C 7. A 8. D

Check the Pronoun (p. 18)
1. incorrect 2. correct 3. incorrect 4. correct
5. incorrect 6. incorrect 7. incorrect 8. incorrect
9. incorrect 10. incorrect 11. correct 12. correct

Find the Verb (p. 19)
1. D 2. B 3. A 4. B 5. A 6. C 7. B 8. B 9. A
10. C 11. C 12. A

Pick the Verb Form (p. 20)
1. a 2. b 3. c 4. a 5. c 6. c 7. c 8. c 9. a
10. b 11. c 12. c

Use Linking Verbs (p. 21)
1. C 2. B 3. D 4. A 5. C 6. A 7. D 8. B

Use the Verb (p. 22)
Evaluate sentences on completion, clarity, and correct usage of the given verb.

Use Verb Tenses (p. 23)
2. break 3. drew 4. hung 5. slept 6. spend
7. leave 8. grown 9. think 10. wrote

Use a Better Verb (p. 24)
Answers will vary.

Find the Adjective (p. 25)
1. C 2. D 3. B 4. B 5. A 6. B 7. C 8. A 9. B
10. B 11. A 12. A 13. D

Make Comparisons (p. 26)
2. youngest 3. larger 4. better 5. worse 6. most
7. luckier 8. hungrier 9. worst 10. flat 11. fewest
12. wetter

Use a Better Adjective (p. 27)
Answers will vary.

Answer with Adverbs (p. 28)
Answers will vary.

Use Adjectives and Adverbs (p. 29)
1. b 2. c 3. a 4. c 5. a 6. a 7. d 8. d

Write Prepositional Phrases (p. 30)
Sentences will vary.

Add Prepositional Phrases (p. 31)
Sentences will vary.

Find Spelling Mistakes (p. 32)
1. A 2. A 3. C 4. B 5. A 6. B 7. B 8. B 9. A
10. C 11. B 12. A

Spell Check (p. 33)
1. easyly 2. charje 3. polise 4. reaktion 5. No
Mistake 6. remane 7. No Mistake 8. sqwish
9. gobbel 10. swetter 11. No Mistake 12. twelfe
13. punnish 14. jingull 15. turky 16. chizzle

Pick the Homophone (p. 34)
1. ax 2. break 3. ceiling 4. chili 5. coarse 6. fare
7. flour 8. hire 9: heard 10. petal 11. wring
12. soar

Write With Homophones (p. 35)
Sentences will vary; evaluate students' writing for clarity, completeness, and correct use of both homophones.

Form Compound Words (p. 36)
1–5. brainstorm, quarterback, screwdriver, strawberry, watercolor 6–10. Sentences will vary; evaluate students' writing for clarity, completeness, and reasonable use of the compound words.

Work With Contractions (p. 37)
2. We are 3. might have 4. it will 5. can not
6. I am 7. would not 8. need not 9. she would
10. you had 11. will not 12. let us

Explain Prefixes (p. 38)
Sentences will vary.

Explain Suffixes (p. 39)
Sentences will vary.

Find Capitalization Errors (p. 40)
1. A 2. B 3. C 4. No Error 5. C 6. B 7. B 8. C
9. B 10. C 11. No Error 12. A

Use Capital Letters (p. 41)
2. O, b, t 3. I, B, v 4. R, t, c 5. t, p, M 6. M, e, t
7. l, D, e 8. K, s, r 9. Y, b, a 10. W, p, o 11. l, A, p
12. e, y, T

End Marks (p. 42)
1. ? 2. ! 3. . 4. ? 5. ! 6. ? 7. . or ! 8. ! 9. ?
10. ! or . 11. . 12. ?

Use the End Mark (p. 43)
Sentences will vary; evaluate for clarity, completeness, and suitable use of end mark.

TEACHER NOTES and SELECTED ANSWERS

Watch the Punctuation (p. 44)
1. B   2. C   3. C   4. A   5. B   6. B   7. A   8. C

Fix Punctuation Errors (p. 45)
1. "Do you want to set up a club house, Fred?" asked Wayne. OR "Do you want to set up a club house?" Fred asked Wayne.   2. Fred pointed to the old tool shed, the one that nobody used anymore.   3. "We could paint it, add rugs and pillows, and hang out there," said Fred.   4. So the boys began to clean out the shed, which took several long, dusty days.   5. "Yuck!" yelled Wayne as he walked through sticky cobwebs.   6. After a few weeks, they barely recognized that old shed.   7. Fred's aunt gave them a rug; Wayne's mom gave them some old pillows.   8. They painted the door to say "F & W Club. Private! Stay Out!"   9. It's amazing how those boys turned that old shed into a perfect hideaway.   10. "Now all we need is room service," joked Wayne.

Part 2: Writing Styles

Continue a Sentence (p. 48)
Sentences will vary; evaluate for continuity, clarity, and completeness.

Write Complete Sentences (p. 49)
Sentences will vary; evaluate for clarity and completeness.

Combine Two Sentences (p. 50)
Sentences may vary.

Fix Run-On Sentences (p. 51)
Corrections may vary.

Avoid Double Negatives (p. 52)
Corrections may vary.

Figure Out the Error (p. 53)
1. C   2. D   3. C   4. B   5. A   6. B   7. D   8. A

Choose the Synonym (p. 54)
1. D   2. A   3. B   4. C   5. A   6. C   7. A   8. D   9. C   10. A

Choose the Antonym (p. 55)
1. A   2. C   3. B   4. D   5. A   6. C   7. B   8. B   9. C   10. D

Use Figures of Speech (p. 56)
1. A   2. D   3. B   4. C   5. C   6. A   7. D   8. B   9. B   10. C

Explain Figures of Speech (p. 57)
Explanations may vary.

Add Supporting Details (p. 58)
Sentences will vary; evaluate for continuity, clarity, and completeness.

Topic Sentence and Support (p. 59)
1. b   2. c   3. a   4. b   5. a   6. c

Unity in Paragraphs (p. 60)
1. Topic sentence: Bridges let travelers cross water, roads, rails, and deep pits safely. Unnecessary sentence: Someone filmed the collapse of the Tacoma Narrows Bridge in 1940.   2. Topic sentence: Bridges can be truly beautiful and graceful. Unnecessary sentence: Hard stone, such as granite, might be used to build a bridge.   3. Topic sentence: Nature itself has sometimes been a fine bridge builder. Unnecessary sentence: National Bridges National Monument is in Utah.   4. Topic sentence: Some bridges need to move so that boats can pass beneath them. Unnecessary sentence: Another name for a drawbridge is a *bascule*.

Use Signal Words (p. 61)
1. D   2. A   3. C   4. C   5. A   6. A   7. B   8. D

Part 3: The Writing Process

Prewriting activities (pp. 64–71)
For open-ended activities, evaluate each in terms of completeness, clarity, cohesion, and students' ability to communicate responses that satisfy the given task.

Prewriting: Fact vs. Opinion (p. 72)
1. O   2. F   3. F   4. O   5. O   6. F   7. F   8. O   9. O   10. F   11. O   12. F   13. O   14. O

Prewriting: Library Resources (1) (p. 73)
1. C   2. C   3. D   4. B   5. B   6. D   7. C   8. D

Prewriting: Library Resources (2) (p. 74)
1. C   2. A   3. A   4. A   5. B   6. C   7. A   8. A

Drafting: Write the Steps (p. 75)
Evaluate each in terms of clarity, order, completeness, and the inclusion of key information.

Drafting: Organize the Sentences (p. 76)
1. C   2. D   3. B   4. A   5. A   6. B   7. C   8. D   9. D   10. C   11. B   12. A   13. A   14. D   15. C   16. B

Drafting: Topic Sentences (p. 77)
Topic sentences will vary; evaluate whether they encompass the given group of sentences.

Drafting: Know Your Audience (p. 78)
Paragraphs will vary; evaluate for order, clarity, completeness, and appropriateness for the given audience.

Drafting: Know Your Purpose (p. 79)
Sentences will vary; evaluate for clarity and appropriateness for the given purpose.

Editing: Choose the Best Sentence (p. 80)
1. B   2. A   3. B   4. C   5. B   6. C   7. C   8. B   9. A   10. B

Editing: Remove Extra Details (p. 81)
1. Dad is picking up...   2. Her trumpet was made...   3. My Uncle Arnold...   4. Other water sports are...

Revising: Fix the Mistakes (p. 82)
1. C   2. B   3. A   4. C   5. A   6. C   7. B   8. C

Revising: Liven Up Dull Sentences (p. 83)
Sentences will vary; evaluate students' ability to improve the sentence while keeping its essential meaning.

Part 4: Writing Activities

Writing Activities (pp. 86–92)
Responses will vary; evaluate each piece of writing in terms of students' ability to convey the required information in a coherent, organized, and clear manner.